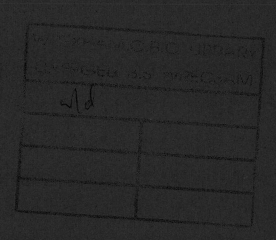

A Painful History of Medicine

Bedpans, Blood + Bandages
a history of hospitals

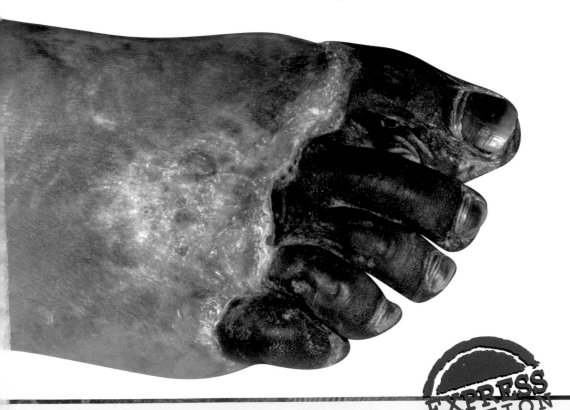

John Townsend

www.raintreepublishers.co.uk
Visit our website to find out more information about **Raintree** books.

To order:
☎ Phone 44 (0) 1865 888113
🖹 Send a fax to 44 (0) 1865 314091
💻 Visit the Raintree bookshop at **www.raintreepublishers.co.uk** to browse our catalogue and order online.

First published in Great Britain by Raintree, Halley Court, Jordan Hill, Oxford OX2 8EJ,
part of Harcourt Education.
Raintree is a registered trademark of Harcourt Education Ltd.

© Harcourt Education Ltd 2006
First published in paperback in 2006
The moral right of the proprietor has been asserted.

Produced for Raintree Publishers by Discovery Books Ltd
Editorial: Carol Usher, Melanie Copland, and Kate Buckingham
Design: Michelle Lisseter, Rob Norridge, and Bridge Creative Services Ltd
Picture Research: Hannah Taylor and Ginny Stroud-Lewis
Production: Duncan Gilbert
Originated by Dot Gradations
Printed and bound in China
by South China Printing Company

ISBN 1 406 20428 5 (hardback)
10 09 08 07 06
10 9 8 7 6 5 4 3 2 1

ISBN 1 406 20433 1 (paperback)
10 09 08 07 06
10 9 8 7 6 5 4 3 2 1

British Library Cataloguing in Publication Data
Townsend, John
Bedpans, blood & bandages : a history of hospitals. Differentiated ed. - (A painful history of medicine)
362.1'1'09
A full catalogue record for this book is available from the British Library.

This levelled text is a version of *Freestyle: A Painful History of Medicine: Bedpans, Blood & Bandages*

Acknowledgements
Alamy Images pp. 36–37 (Popperfoto), 42 (David Wall), 45 (Steve Allen, Brand X Pictures), 48–49 (AGStockUSA, Inc. Ed Young), 48 (Comstock Images); Art Directors and Trip pp. 13, 17; Corbis pp. 10–11 (Underwood & Underwood), 11 (Sygma/ Jacques Langevin), 12 (Historical Picture Archive), 12–13 (Anthony Bannister/ Gallo Images), 14 (Michael Nicholson), 14–15, 16–17 (Michael Maslan Historic Photographs), 18–19, 26 (Peter Turnley), 26–27 (Hulton-Deutsch Collection), 32 (Bettmann), 34, 37 (Swim Ink), 38–39 (Tim Fisher/ The Military Picture Library), 39 (Bettmann), 40 (Kit Kittle), 41 (Yann Arthus-Bertrand), 42–43 (Jonathan Blair), 44–45 (Dusko Despotovic); Getty Images pp. 50–51; Hulton Archive pp. 31, 33, 38; Mary Evans Picture Library pp. 23, 24, 25, 29; Medical on Line pp. 6, 22–23; Science Photo Library pp. 19 (National Library of Medicine), 20 (Sinclair Stammers), 20–21 (Jean-Loup Charmet), 21 (Mike Devlin), 43 (Ed Young), 46 (Cal Goetgheluck), 46–47 (Volker Steger), 47 (Geoff Tompkinson); Sylvia Cordaiy p. 15; The Art Archive/ Imperial War Museum, London pp. 34–35; The Kobal Collection pp. 6–7 (MGM), 8–9 (Dreamworks/ Universal/ Buitendijk, Jaap), 30, 50; The Royal College of Surgeons pp. 4–5; Topham Picturepoint p. 28; Wellcome Library, London pp. 9, 30–31, 35.

Cover photograph of patients lined up in a ward reproduced with permission of Corbis

Contents

Any words appearing in the text in bold **like this**, are explained in the glossary. You can also look out for them in the Word bank at the bottom of each page.

Hospitals used to be terrible places. They had filthy rats and messy **bedpans**. Bandages were dirty. Patients' wounds became infected. They oozed with slimy **pus.** The smells were disgusting. Hospitals would make you feel sick. People were afraid to go to the hospital. They might not come out alive.

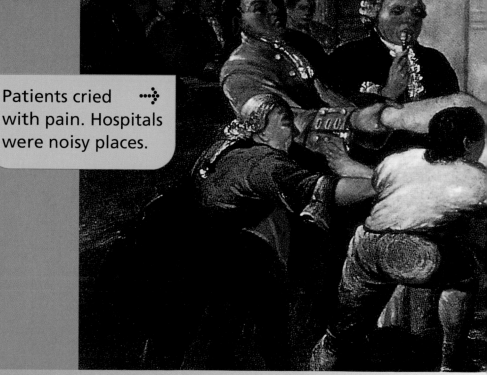

Patients cried with pain. Hospitals were noisy places.

Word bank   bedpan   shallow pan used as a toilet by someone in bed

Times have changed

Hospitals have come a long way since those days! Doctors have learned a lot over the past thousand years. Doctors and nurses use the latest equipment. Heart and lung machines are up to date pieces of equipment. They can treat very ill people.

Hospitals still have bedpans, bandages, and blood. But now hospitals save lives.

Find out later...

...why there were rats in hospitals.

...why some hospitals were in fields.

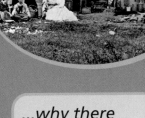

...why there are maggots in hospitals.

pus   thick, yellow-green, smelly liquid made by infected wounds

Today, hospitals are places where sick people can get better. But hospitals have only been like this for a short time. Things were different in Greek and Roman times.

Greeks in the past

The ancient Greeks cared for sick people at home. If the sick person was lucky, a "healer" might visit. Healers used honey or herbs as medicine. There was little proper medical care.

Nowhere to go

Thousands of years ago there were no special places to nurse sick people. Hospitals were not built until after Roman times. Hospitals are a very new idea.

This patient has a boil. Greeks and Romans often cut boils open. ⁙

Romans in the past

The Romans looked after their health. They thought clean water, clean bodies, and exercise were good for them. They were right!

The Romans had many slaves. Slaves sometimes fell ill. Then they often had to look after themselves. But some slave-owners built rooms for sick slaves. They paid doctors to care for them.

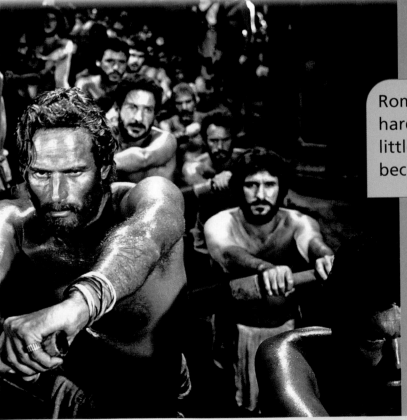

Roman slaves had hard lives. They had little help if they became ill.

Roman soldiers

Roman soldiers were often hurt in battles. They were often left behind to die.

Augustus was a Roman **emperor**. He ruled after Julius Caesar. He had a huge army. Augustus built hospitals for his soldiers. They were large halls in **forts**. He did this to look after the **injured** soldiers in his army. Ordinary people had nowhere to go when they were sick.

Roman Empire

Julius Caesar was the first emperor in the Roman empire. In 55 BC, over 2,000 years ago, he invaded Britain.

Gladiators often got hurt. Then they needed nursing.

Word bank   **fort**   building that can stand up to enemy attack

Fighting wounds

The Romans trained men to fight each other with weapons. These men were called **gladiators**. The Romans paid gladiators to fight. The Romans liked to watch them.

Often gladiators were hurt. Then they were cared for in hospitals. Doctors put their insides back and stitched them up.

This sculpture shows an injured gladiator.

Roman hospitals

Romans built hospitals in forts. You can still see ruins or remains of hospitals. Historians have dug up the ruins and found medical instruments. We have learned a lot about Roman hospitals this way.

gladiator person trained to fight with weapons. Gladiators were paid to fight in ancient Roman shows.

Early Christians

Jerusalem is a city in Israel. This is where Jesus Christ lived. He taught people to care for the poor and sick. Followers of Jesus Christ are called **Christians**.

Christians built places where ill people could be treated. This was the start of hospitals for everyone.

Rest houses

Christians set up **hostels** in many countries. Hostels are a cheap place for travellers to stay. Sick people went to them too. They were given care and rest.

This is a hospital outside Jerusalem in the 1900s.

Word bank · **surgery** operating on the body, using knives and other tools, to treat injuries and illness

The first big hospitals

About 1,500 years ago, in AD 550, some hospitals were quite large. There was a big hospital in Jerusalem with 200 beds. Some hospitals were bigger still. They were in Greece. These even did **surgery**.

Caring for the sick is part of many **religions**. **Islam** is a religion like this. People who follow Islam are called **Muslims**. They believe in caring for the body. Muslims built hospitals too.

Hospitals in the Middle East

Syria is in the Middle East. The Muslims built their first hospital there. It opened in AD 707, about 1,300 years ago. Muslims kept building hospitals. By the year 1200, there were over 35 hospitals.

This is a modern hospital. It is in Saudi Arabia.

religion   set of beliefs that people follow

The **Middle Ages** was a time in history. It was 500 to 1,500 years ago. There were lots of new ideas about medicine then.

Monks in the Middle Ages

Monks grew plants to make medicines. They cared for sick monks in special rooms. Monks looked after sick, weak, and old people.

Blood

People thought letting blood out of a vein would make sick people better! The ancient Greeks did this. This carried on until recent times.

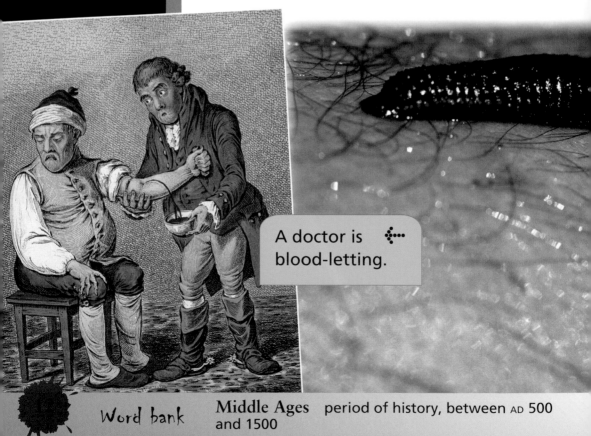

A doctor is blood-letting.

Word bank | **Middle Ages** period of history, between AD 500 and 1500

Blood-letting

Sometimes monks cut patients' arms. They let the blood drain into a bowl. This is called **blood-letting**. They thought that having too much blood caused illnesses.

Sometimes **leeches** were used to suck blood from a patient's body. The leeches slowly swelled up with blood.

Blood-letting could be dangerous. It could make sick people even weaker.

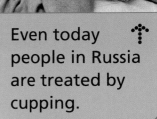

Even today people in Russia are treated by cupping.

Cupping

Cupping was done to draw away **infected** blood. Warm cups were pushed onto cut skin. The blood was then collected in the cups.

This leech is ready to drink some blood.

monk   man who devotes himself to God and lives in a monastery

City hospitals

There were hospitals in Europe from the 12th **century**. They were built in cities. **Monks** and nuns ran them. There were strict rules.

When patients went into hospital, their clothes were washed and mended. Often patients had to go to bed without any clothes. Sometimes they had to share a bed with someone else.

This is St John's hospital in Bruges, Belgium. It was built in 1188. It was one of the oldest hospitals in Europe. It is now a hospital museum.

Rats ran around patients in many hospitals.

ward   room in a hospital, often for a certain type of patient

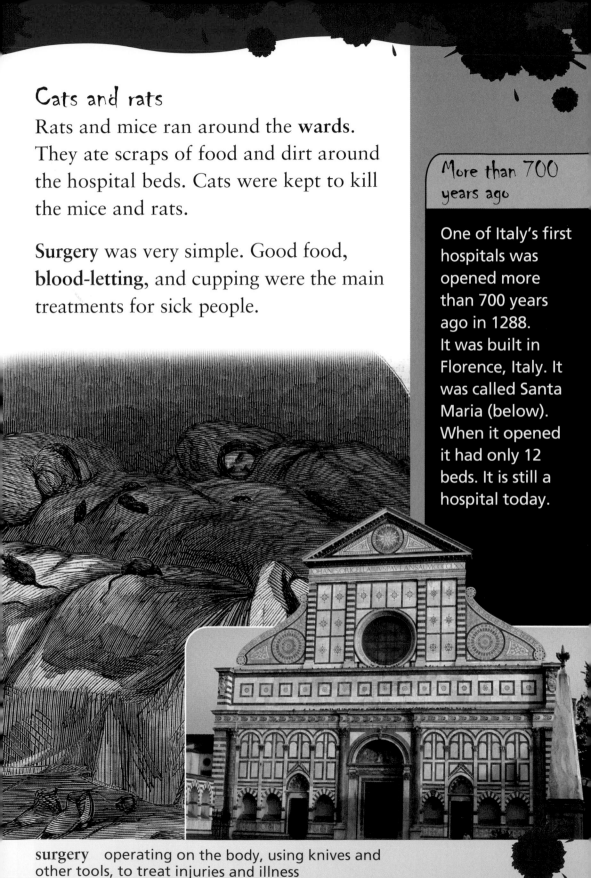

Cats and rats

Rats and mice ran around the **wards**. They ate scraps of food and dirt around the hospital beds. Cats were kept to kill the mice and rats.

Surgery was very simple. Good food, **blood-letting,** and cupping were the main treatments for sick people.

More than 700 years ago

One of Italy's first hospitals was opened more than 700 years ago in 1288. It was built in Florence, Italy. It was called Santa Maria (below). When it opened it had only 12 beds. It is still a hospital today.

surgery operating on the body, using knives and other tools, to treat injuries and illness

Leprosy

Leprosy was a terrible skin disease. There used to be no cure. Victims' skin became scaly and **infected**. Their noses, fingers, and toes broke off. **Lepers** often went blind too.

It is very easy to catch leprosy. It is very **infectious**. People were very scared of being close to lepers. Lepers had to warn people that they had leprosy. They had to shave their heads and wear a yellow cross. Lepers rang a bell and shouted "unclean".

The dreaded disease

People thought that lepers were evil. They shouted names or threw stones at them. Lepers were made to live away from other people.

Lepers had to beg for food. ┈┈▶

Word bank   infectious   spreads easily from one person to another

Asylums

About a thousand years ago, in the year AD 1000, there was an outbreak of leprosy. It spread quickly through Europe. This was an **epidemic**. It lasted over 200 years.

After 100 years, people with leprosy were put in leper houses, or **asylums**. Asylums were built outside towns. They gave shelter and food to the lepers. But there was not much medical help.

This girl has leprosy. She is covered in sores.

Cure for leprosy

In 1873 the cause of leprosy was found. This was a type of **bacteria**. These tiny living things can cause disease. A cure was found in the 1940s.

epidemic   outbreak of a disease that spreads over a wide area

Human zoo

In 1247 a hospital for "lunatics" was started. It was in London. Patients were kept in cages. People paid to stare at them. It was like a zoo.

Before 1800, life in hospital was hard. You would get a bed to rest in and meals. But treatments, like **surgery** and drugs, were risky. You might not get better.

Bacteria are tiny living things. They can cause disease. Bacteria spread easily between patients. They grew in patients' wounds. Bacteria made poisons. They could kill. Doctors had to chop off infected arms and legs.

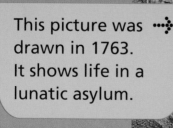

This picture was drawn in 1763. It shows life in a lunatic asylum.

Word bank

bacteria tiny living thing that can cause illness or disease

Mental illness

Sometimes our brains do not quite work as they should. This can be because of stress or disease. We may need to be treated for **mental illness.**

Over 200 years ago, people with mental illness were kept in **lunatic asylums.** These were also known as "madhouses". Some asylums tried to help patients. Many did not.

The calming chair

People thought that mental illness was caused by devils. Benjamin Rush thought it was a disease of the mind. He was one of the first to believe this. He made the calming chair (below).

People with mental illness were put in the calming chair. This kept them still.

lunatic   old-fashioned name given to a person with mental illness

Misery

In the 1600s and 1700s many new hospitals were built in Europe. But the hospitals could not cope when **plague** struck. This is a type of deadly disease that spreads quickly.

The hospitals became very crowded. The beds were filthy and full of fleas. Many patients died. No one knew then that the fleas spread the plague when they bit people.

Hospital beds were very itchy places. Fleas and bedbugs lived in the bedding.

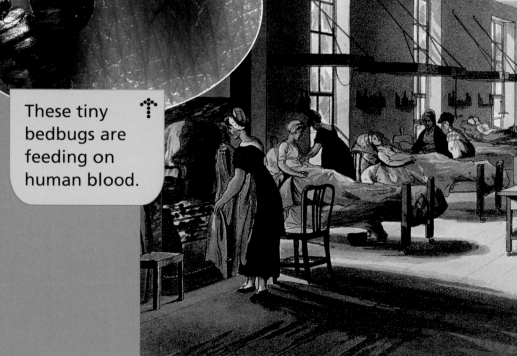

These tiny bedbugs are feeding on human blood.

Word bank plague deadly disease that spreads very quickly

Not enough beds

In 1630, a terrible plague hit Italy. Thousands of people were sent to the hospital in Milan. It had only 280 beds! Sometimes there were five people in a bed.

A great plague hit London in 1665. London had only two hospitals at the time. They filled up very quickly. Victims had to go to the leprosy **asylums** instead.

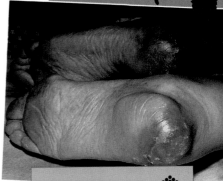

This patient has bedsores.

Bedsores

Sometimes a patient has to stay in bed for a long time. The bed and blankets press on the skin. This can cause bedsores.

Bedsores can get **infected**. Then they seep **pus**. Yet another misery!

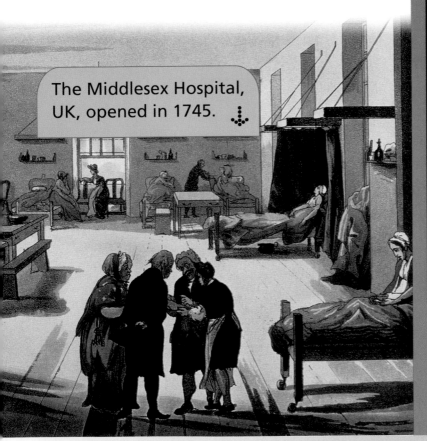

The Middlesex Hospital, UK, opened in 1745.

pus   thick, yellow-green, smelly liquid made by infected wounds

A hospital in the United States

The first hospital in the United States was the Pennsylvania Hospital. It opened in 1751. Benjamin Franklin and Dr Thomas Bond set it up. The hospital was "to care for the sick and **insane**".

Surgery

In the 1800s, surgeons began to operate on patients. It was very risky. **Gangrene** often set in. This happens when **infection** blocks off the blood supply. Then the flesh dies and rots.

Mystery fever

Doctors and nurses did not wash their hands or wash their instruments. This led to infection and illness. This was called **ward** fever. It was caused by **bacteria**. But nobody knew this then.

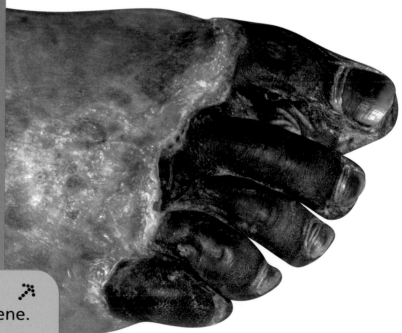

This foot has gangrene.

Word bank   **bacteria**   tiny living thing that can cause illness or disease

Pain

Patients were awake when they were cut open. They were strapped down and given a rag to bite on. The shock, pain, and bleeding would probably kill them.

Anaesthetics were first used in the 1840s. They sent patients to sleep and made the pain less. This made operations safer.

Breakthrough

Joseph Lister was a surgeon. He noticed that many patients died after **surgery**. This was because their wounds went **septic**. They became **infected** with bacteria. This killed the patients.

In 1865 Lister used **antiseptic**. He found the wounds healed quickly and safely.

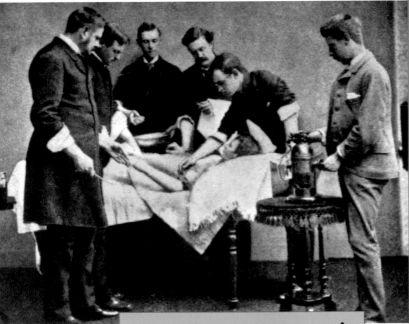

This is an operation in the late 1800s. They are using an antiseptic spray.

septic   infected with bacteria

Nurses

In the 1800s, nursing was hard work. Nurses cleared up messes. They washed the patients. They changed stinking bandages. It was smelly work. Nurses had little training. They were often treated like servants. They were not paid very much.

Sisters were more respected. They ran the **wards** and did the paperwork. Even so, hospital work was not thought of as a good job.

outpatient patient who goes to hospital for treatment but does not stay there

Doctors

In the early 1800s all doctors were men. Elizabeth Blackwell was the first woman doctor. At first she was not allowed to train. But in the end, she studied in New York. She passed all her exams in 1849.

Twenty years later, the first female doctor worked in England. Her name was Elizabeth Garrett Anderson. She opened the first hospital for women.

Students

In the 1800s hospitals did more than care for the sick. They started to teach. **Student** doctors helped in the hospitals. They watched the operations.

Students and nurses discuss a patient in a New York hospital in 1891.

student   person who is learning

Children's hospitals

Very few hospitals looked after children in the 1800s. Poor children lived in damp, dirty houses. They had little food. Many children died from disease. Many babies did not even reach one year old.

In 1852 the first hospital for children opened. It was called the London Hospital for Sick Children.

Children today

A special hospital for children is in London, England. It is called the Great Ormond Street Hospital. This hospital treats 100,000 children every year.

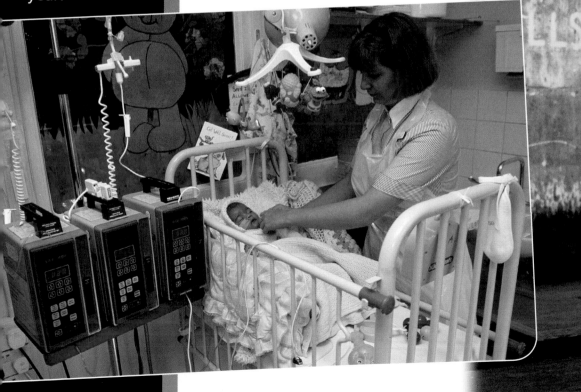

Giving birth

During the 1920s, giving birth was very risky. Babies were born at home. A **midwife** helped at the birth. Many women died giving birth. This was partly because midwives were badly trained.

Today, most babies are born in hospitals. They have special **wards** where babies are born and looked after. They are called **maternity units**.

Progress

In 1899, a young boy died of a fever. He lived in Seattle, United States. There were no hospitals for him to go to.

His mother tried to put this right. In the end a local hospital agreed to set aside a small ward for children. This grew to be the Children's Hospital of Seattle.

FUW 548

maternity unit   ward in a hospital where babies are born and looked after

Lady with the lamp

Florence Nightingale (below) cared for wounded soldiers. She walked around hospital wards at night. She used an oil lamp to find her way around. The soldiers called her "the lady with the lamp".

Many people are killed or **injured** in wars. **Field hospitals** are set up close to the battlefields. Doctors and nurses are often asked to work in field hospitals.

Crimean War

Turkey fought a war against Russia. There were battles in an area of Russia called the Crimea. The field hospitals were very short of staff and supplies.

field hospital   hospital near a battlefield, often in a tent

Florence Nightingale

A British nurse went to the Crimea to help. She was called Florence Nightingale. She cared for the sick and wounded soldiers. There were about 2,000 of them. They lay in dirty **wards**. Florence and her nurses cleaned the wards up.

After six months the death rate dropped. It came down from 40 per cent to 2 per cent. Florence came home in 1856. She was greeted as a **heroine**.

Mary Seacole

Mary Seacole (below) also went to the Crimean War. She was born in Jamaica. She went to the battle sites to help. She learned how to care for the sick. The soldiers in the Crimea called her Mother Seacole.

heroine female who is admired for her achievements

The American Civil War

In the 1860s, there was a **civil war** in North America. The Northern states fought against the Southern states.

In that war 600,000 men were killed. About 75 per cent of them died in field hospitals. Their wounds or disease had killed them.

Doctors only knew one way to treat a bad leg. They cut it off!

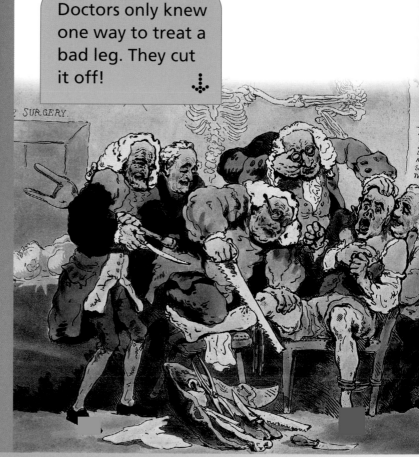

civil war   when soldiers from the same country fight each other

A grim business

In the American Civil War, many of the injuries were from guns. Taking out bullets was a messy job. Doctors often made wounds worse. They did not wash their hands or their tools. They caused even more **infections**.

About 2,000 of the nurses were women. Nurses had to clean and bandage the bullet wounds. Often the wounds were full of **pus** and smelled bad.

"The first thing our surgeon did was to put his finger into the wound, without even washing. Next he used a dirty probe. The patient died a day or two later."

Charles Johnson, aged 18

This is a field hospital during the American Civil War.

first aid help given to a sick or injured person at the scene

The first meeting of the Red Cross was in 1863. It was held in Switzerland, Europe. The Red Cross sign is similar to the Swiss flag. The Swiss flag is a white cross on a red background.

The Red Cross

Doctors and nurses wanted to help those injured in wars. But it was risky to give medical help. If doctors went on to battlefields, they could be shot.

In 1863, a group of doctors and nurses made a sign. The sign was to show soldiers who they were. They used a red cross on a white background. It means medical help.

This is a Red Cross blood unit in World War 2. The sailors are giving blood.

American Red Cross

Clara Barton became a nurse when the American Civil War started. She went to care for the wounded on both sides. After the war she went to Europe. There she learned about the Red Cross. She came back to the United States and started the American Red Cross. This was in 1881.

Spanish–American War

The Red Cross sent emergency supplies to the Spanish-American War of 1868. These helped nurses to save lives. The Red Cross has done this important job ever since. Red Cross supplies go all over the world.

Red Cross nurses did vital work during World War 2.

In World War 1 doctors had to cut off many wounded soldiers' arms and legs. **Anaesthetics** made treatment less painful. **Antiseptics** helped cut down the risk of **infection**.

World War 1

World War 1 lasted from 1914 to 1918. No war before had killed so many people. Eight million soldiers died.

Battles were fought on the fields of France and Belgium. The soldiers dug **trenches.** They used these to shelter from enemy attack. The trenches were very cold and muddy. A lot of soldiers died in the trenches. But even more died in **field hospitals.**

These are Canadian soldiers in France, in 1916.

trench   ditch dug by soldiers. Used as a shelter from enemy attack.

Field hospitals

Many countries fought in World War 1. They all had field hospitals. But they were all grim places.

There were terrible wounds and cries of pain. There were not enough doctors and nurses. There was mud, **trench fever**, and the smell of death.

A nurse and doctor look after a patient. They are in France in 1914.

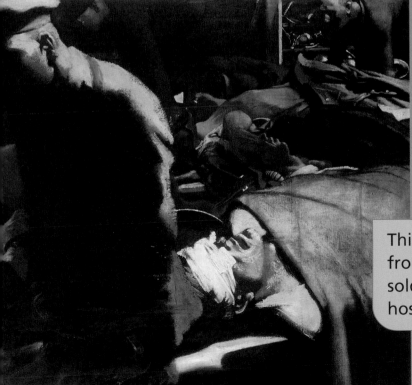

This painting from 1918 shows soldiers in a field hospital.

trench fever   disease that spread in the trenches

World War 2

In World War 2, nobody was safe. Aircraft dropped bombs on towns as well as on soldiers. Often hospitals found it hard to cope.

Field hospitals were in tents or spare buildings. Doctors and nurses were in short supply. Nurses collected rainwater for washing and drinking. Some nurses did not have enough **bedpans** or bowls. Then they would use soldiers' helmets.

Front line

Doctors and nurses knew far more. They had better drugs and equipment. Wounded soldiers had a better chance of staying alive in World War 2 than in World War 1.

A patient is being treated in a field hospital in 1942.

Word bank   malaria   disease that causes fever and chills. It is spread by mosquitoes.

Disease

Soldiers also got **malaria**. This disease causes fever and chills. It is spread by mosquitoes. Hospitals had to help soldiers with malaria as well as war wounds. Nurses lined the tents with mosquito nets. This helped stop the disease spreading. Even so, doctors and nurses still fell ill.

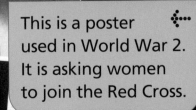

This is a poster used in World War 2. It is asking women to join the Red Cross.

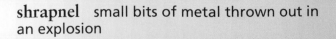

shrapnel small bits of metal thrown out in an explosion

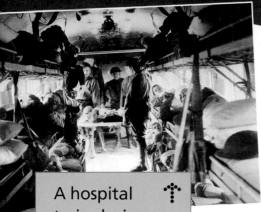

A hospital train during World War 1. About 400 patients were aboard each train.

On the move

In wars, hospitals that move from place to place are vital. These are **mobile** hospitals. All major wars have used them. Soldiers are moved away from danger and treated at the same time.

There have been mobile hospitals for a long time. The Spanish sent a large fleet of warships to attack Britain in 1588. It had hospital ships staffed with 85 doctors.

Wards on wheels

In World War 1 hospital trains had carriages filled with beds. They were like **wards**. They also had a room for operations. The wounded could be treated on the move.

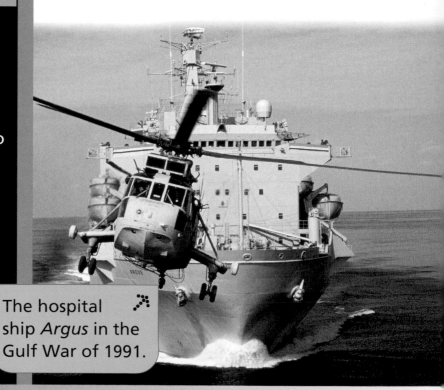

The hospital ship *Argus* in the Gulf War of 1991.

Word bank   **mobile** can be moved from one place to another

State of the art

Today, the US Navy has two hospital ships. They are called *Mercy* and *Comfort*. They are huge. They were built in the 1980s. They were used in wars such as the Gulf War of 1991.

Each ship has 1,000 beds. There are 12 operating rooms and 9 lifts. The ships have helicopter decks. This is where helicopters land with the wounded. Hospital ships have changed a lot since 1588!

Quick exit

The US Army used helicopters in the Vietnam War (1954–1975). They flew soldiers to field hospitals. Doctors treated them on the way. These soldiers had a better chance of staying alive.

This is a hospital helicopter. It is rescuing soldiers in the Vietnam War in 1969.

Today, most of us can get to our nearest hospital easily. But some people live a very long way from a hospital. These days hospitals can go to them.

Australia

Some parts of Australia are huge distances away from hospitals. These areas are called the **outback**. If people fell ill there, they used to be in big trouble. The nearest hospital could be days away.

Flying doctors

Australia has a special ambulance service. It has planes that are like mini hospitals. The planes even have their own doctors. They take to the air every day and save many lives.

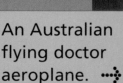

An Australian flying doctor aeroplane. ⋯⋗

Word bank   outback   large area a long way from a town

Flying doctor

Australia has a flying-doctor service. It brings hospital support to the most out-of-the-way areas by aeroplane. This saves hundreds of lives each year.

In the 1990s a family went camping in the outback. Their son, Ryan, could not breathe. An **infection** had blocked his windpipe. His parents called the flying doctor. A plane flew Ryan to a hospital in Perth, Australia. Ryan is now a fit and healthy young man.

The African bush

Most of East Africa is desert and bush. People have to travel a long way to reach a hospital. Luckily, there is the East Africa Flying Doctor Service. It can get to sick people quickly.

A flying doctor in Kenya.

infection   disease caused by tiny living things, like bacteria

Air ambulance

Most countries have **remote** areas far from a hospital. People often need rescuing from the mountains or the sea. Helicopters are able to reach these places. They are called air ambulances.

Helicopters can rescue people from hard-to-reach places. Air ambulances have up-to-date medical equipment on board. They carry highly trained nurses. Air ambulances save many lives.

The *Life Flight NZ* air ambulance.

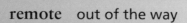

Word bank   remote   out of the way

2003: LIGHTNING STRIKES CLIMBERS IN UNITED STATES

Disaster struck on Grand Teton peak in Wyoming. Lightning killed one climber; two others were thrown off the peak. They were badly burned and hung by ropes from a cliff.

One climber used a mobile phone to call for help. An air ambulance rushed to the scene. The climbers had emergency **first aid** treatment in the helicopter. Then they were taken to the hospital in Salt Lake City. Fast action saved their lives.

Inside an air ambulance.

A rock climber with a broken foot is rescued by helicopter.

intensive care   ward or area where dangerously ill people are given special care

Emergency

People are often **injured** far from hospitals. But usually, they can still have treatment for their injuries.

In 2001, eight-year-old Jessie Arbogast was swimming in the sea. A large shark bit off his arm. Jessie's uncle and a park ranger pulled the arm from the shark's throat. They put it in ice. **Paramedics** came quickly. They flew Jessie to hospital. Doctors sewed Jessie's arm back on. It took 11 hours. Jessie lived and has both arms.

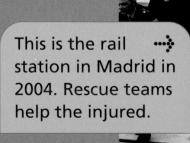

This is the rail station in Madrid in 2004. Rescue teams help the injured.

Word bank   **paramedic** emergency worker who gives first aid before a person gets to hospital

Bomb attack

Sometimes terrible events happen. In 2004, **terrorists** planted bombs in trains in Madrid. They blew up and killed nearly 200 people. Thousands more were **injured**. Hospitals had to act quickly.

Before long 1,300 emergency workers were helping victims. Ambulances rushed the wounded to hospital. People gave blood. Hospitals were at breaking point. But they saved thousands of lives.

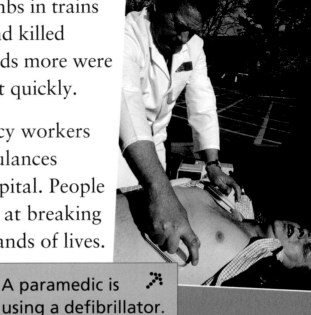

A paramedic is using a defibrillator.

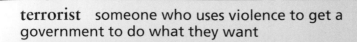

First aid

If the heart stops, the brain does not get enough blood and oxygen. Now, we have a machine that can start the heart again. It is called a **defibrillator**. It shocks the heart to get it beating.

terrorist someone who uses violence to get a government to do what they want

Maggots

Imagine you are in hospital. You wake up and see maggots. They are wriggling out of your flesh! This would probably be quite a shock!

Maggots are used in hospitals today. Maggots do your body no harm. They leave healthy flesh alone. Maggots eat dead flesh. They kill the **bacteria** and stop **infection**. This allows the injury to heal.

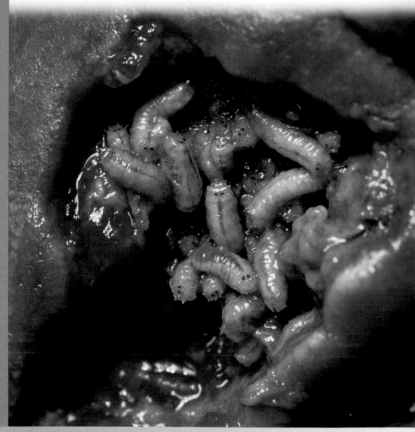

clot   form into a thick lump

Blood-suckers

Doctors have used leeches for 2500 years. Leeches suck blood. They drink up to five times their own body weight.

Leeches also make a chemical. This stops blood forming lumps or **clotting**. This can help a patient's blood flow around the body better.

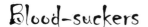

Leeches have been used in hospitals for centuries.

ulcer   open sore, often full of pus

Another world

We have seen what hospitals used to be like. Today they are very different. They have very advanced equipment. Some machines scan our bodies. They can tell us what is going on inside.

Very ill people can stay in **intensive care**. These hospital **wards** are where they get special care. A patient can be plugged into a life-support machine. This runs a patient's body for him. Then doctors treat the problem.

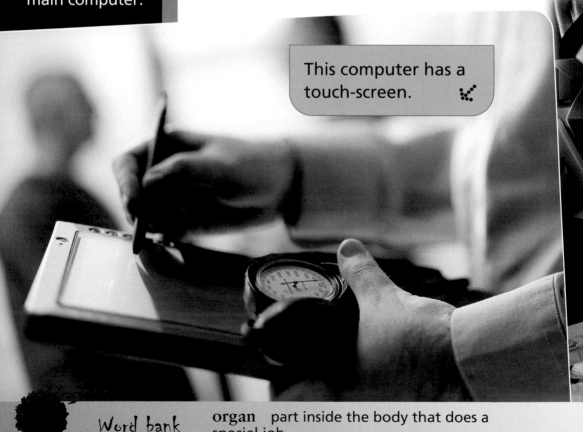

This computer has a touch-screen.

Word bank   **organ**   part inside the body that does a special job

In the news

Today people can go to hospitals anywhere. They can travel across the world to get the best treatment. A baby from Italy was very ill. Her main **organs** were failing. She went to stay in a hospital in Florida, United States. There she had an operation to replace them.

The operation took 12 hours. She had 8 new organs in all. She would have died without this special surgery.

Tomorrow's world

In the future, patients will have a computer by their bedsides. Everything will be **digital**. This means all the notes will be stored on a computer.

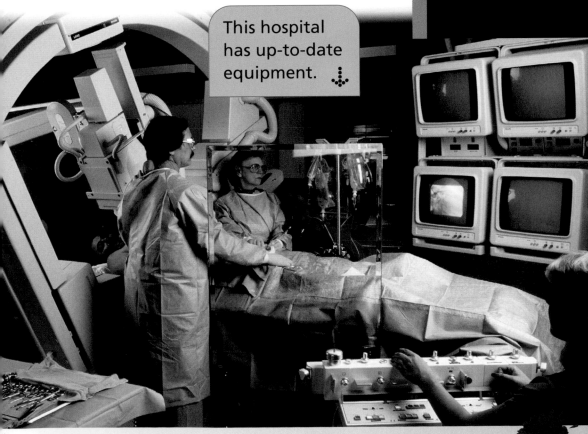

This hospital has up-to-date equipment.

digital   storing information on computers

Hospital drama

People like to know what goes on in hospitals. Many TV programmes are made about hospitals. A lot of people watch them.

ER (Emergency Room) is a TV show. It is about life in an American hospital. This programme is very popular around the world. The actors working on *ER* are paid much more money than real doctors and nurses.

This is the actor Robin Williams. He is playing a hospital clown in the film *Patch Adams*.

New world

Real life is often more incredible than a TV drama. Imagine being asleep for 20 years and then waking up in hospital.

This really happened to one man in the United States. In 2003, Terry Wallis woke up after 19 years in a coma. He was 38 years old. He was only 19 years old when he was in a car crash. He is still learning about the modern world.

No real change

Hospitals will keep on changing. But some things will stay the same. There will still be bedpans, bandages, and blood!

Another day's work for the stars of *ER*.

Did you know?

Books

Clara Barton, Christy Devillier (Buddy Books, 2004)

Great Inventions: Medicine, Paul Dowswell (Heinemann Library, 2001)

The Life and World of: Florence Nightingale, Struan Reid (Heinemann Library, 2003)

Using the Internet

The Internet can tell you more about medicine through the ages. You can use a search engine, such as www.yahooligans.com.
Type in keywords such as:

- leech
- Florence Nightingale
- gladiators

Search tips

There are billions of pages on the Internet. It can be difficult to find what you are looking for.

These search tips will help you find useful websites more quickly:

- Know exactly what you want to find out about.
- Use two to six keywords in a search. Put the most important word first.
- Only use names of people, places, or things.

Where to search

Search engine
A search engine looks through through millions of website pages. It lists all the sites that match the words in the search box. You will find the best matches are at the top of the list, on the first page.

Search directory
A person instead of a computer has sorted a search directory. You can search by keyword or subject and browse through the different sites. It is like looking through books on a library shelf.

Glossary

anaesthetic drug to make patients sleep or treatments less painful

antiseptic substance that stops harmful bacteria growing and spreading disease

asylum place where people can find shelter and be safe

bacteria tiny living thing that can cause illness or disease

bedpan shallow pan used as a toilet by someone in bed

blood-letting cutting the skin or a vein to let blood flow out

century one hundred years

Christian person who follows Jesus Christ and his teachings

civil war when soldiers from the same country fight each other

clot form into a thick lump

defibrillator machine that starts a heart working. It shocks the heart muscles after they have stopped.

digital storing information on computers

emperor ruler of an empire

epidemic outbreak of a disease that spreads over a wide area

field hospital hospital near a battlefield, often in a tent

first aid help given to a sick or injured person at the scene

fort building that can stand up to enemy attack

gangrene when flesh rots and dies. This is due to lack of blood supply that can be caused by infection.

gladiator person trained to fight with weapons. Gladiators were paid to fight in ancient Roman shows.

heroine female who is admired for her achievements

hostel cheap place for travellers

infect when micro-organisms get into a person and cause disease

infection disease caused by tiny living things, like bacteria

infectious spreads easily from one person to another

insane mad, or seriously mentally ill

injure hurt or damage

intensive care ward or area where dangerously ill patients are given special care

Islam religion based on the teachings of Muhammad

Latin language used by the Romans

leech flat worm that sucks blood

leper person suffering from leprosy. Leprosy is a terrible skin disease.

lunatic old-fashioned name given to a person with mental illness

malaria disease that causes fever and chills. It is spread by mosquitoes.

maternity unit ward in a hospital where babies are born and looked after

mental illness when the brain is not working properly

Middle Ages period of history, between about AD 500 and 1500

midwife nurse who helps women in childbirth

mobile can be moved from one place to another

monastery place where monks live

monk man who devotes himself to God and lives in a monastery

Muslim follower of the religion Islam

organ part inside the body that does a special job

outback large area a long way from a town

outpatient patient who goes to hospital for treatment but does not stay there

paramedic emergency worker who gives first aid before a person gets to hospital

plague deadly disease that spreads very quickly

pus thick, yellow-green, smelly liquid made by infected wounds

religion set of beliefs that people follow

remote out of the way

septic infected with bacteria

shrapnel small bits of metal thrown out in an explosion

student person who is learning

surgery operating on the body, using knives and other tools, to treat injuries and illness

terrorist someone who uses violence to get a government to do what they want

trench ditch dug by soldiers. Used as a shelter from enemy attack.

trench fever disease that spread in the trenches

ulcer open sore, often full of pus

ward room in a hospital, often for a certain type of patient

Index

Titles in the *A Painful History of Medicine* series include:

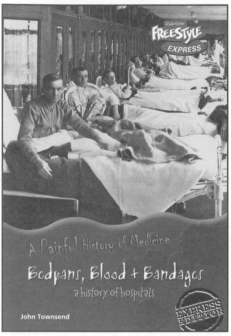

Hardback   1 406 20428 5

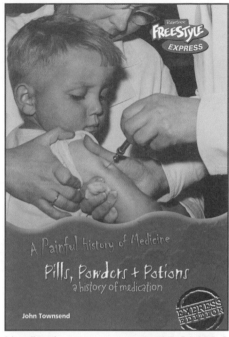

Hardback   1 406 20429 3

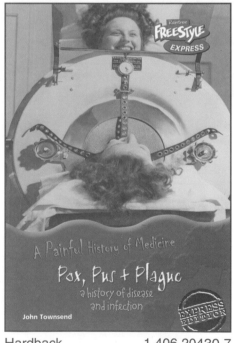

Hardback   1 406 20430 7

Hardback   1 406 20431 5

Find out about other Freestyle Express titles on our website www.raintreepublishers.co.uk